FIGHTING TO
WIN

EDITION ONE

DELATRON JOHNSON

√asteland Press
www.wastelandpress.net
Shelbyville, KY USA

Fighting to Win:
Edition One
by Delatron Johnson

First Printing – June 2014
Paperback ISBN: 978-1-60047-966-3
e-mail: Deljohnson03@yahoo.com

Unless otherwise indicated, all scripture quotations are taken from
The King James Version of the Bible

Printed in the United States of America

0   1   2   3   4

INTRODUCTION

S itting here thinking, wondering and dreaming what life would have been like 34 years ago if I had been born to a different mother and father, born into a different family or not born at all is a question that has always been a mystery to me.

I was born December 24, 1979 and to most the birth of a child is such a blessing. It's something that most mothers, fathers and loved ones look forward to such a blessing. Such a sweet bundle of joy to have entered into the lives of those who look forward to showering with love, affection, dreams and aspirations that one day that new little bundle of joy will make everyone proud.

Oh how I would love to know what that feels like. How I wish that being born would have made everyone smile, hug, cherish, and look forward to life's blessings that this sweet bundle of joy would have brought into their lives. Born to a mother who had already had a baby girl I guess that put this baby girl in second place for her love and affection or was it that? Born to a father that had a wife and daughter on the way definitely put this little girl in last place and who knew that for years to come I would have to fight my way to his heart. Well my story only gets better from here so sit back and take this journey through my life with me.

CHAPTER ONE

My life, as I knew it, was what I thought life should be. The drugs, the yelling, the abuse, both mentally and physically; the running from authorities, to living with friends for days at a time to coming home to food that was being cooked and sold for drugs. This was normal for this 10 year old little girl. My mom had been addicted to crack cocaine since before I was born, and to this day she battles the sickness. Despite several opportunities for change, changed have not known her by name.

The environment I grew up in affected my life to a great degree. I had to break free from this prison; grab my life by the horns and run in a better direction. Eventually, I did that. However, the better direction didn't meet me without a fight to live. I had to fight my way through the storm to win. As I begin to recall some of my life's experiences, I've been told that I've emotionally blocked the pain because I really didn't remember much before the age of 10. However, I do know that I used to try to figure out ways to block images and words from my life, period, because at times the pain was just unbearable. I've talked to several people, some were family members and others were friends of my mom, and it still doesn't make sense to me. These people were there! They saw me and what I've endured. They've told me stories and it's still a blur to me.

Every now and then, I wish I could turn back the hands of time and look over my life like I was watching a movie. I imagine I'd watch it over and over again until it made sense. Well, since that is not possible, I would take what I have been told, the information I'd been given, and put the fitting pieces together like a puzzle. I was thinking, maybe, just maybe it will all come back. It never did. The pain only intensified when I thought about it because I couldn't understand any of it. From what I've been told, it appears that I was a happy little girl. I've heard stories of how my mom took great care of us. I've seen pictures where I looked really happy. I was dressed real nice, my hair was done, and I was smiling in every picture. But, why can't I remember any of that? Why is it such a blur? How did those memories go away? How did I go from smiling and laughing to trying to find my smile and hear my laughter? The things I can recall before age 10 is living with my mom and sister, often having people indulging with her in drug activity with her, sprawled out around the house with empty cigarette boxes, beer cans, and pipes just lying around.

With all this, I also, very clearly, recall having "THE" definite answer to block all pain. And, the only thing I thought, that was a definite solution, was suicide. At the time, when my little sister was two years younger than I, we were very close. So, from time to time, when I thought life was treating me good, I would push my suicidal thoughts to the back of my mind. I also had an elder sister that lived with my grandmother. I always felt that she had her family, which consisted of my grandmother, and my aunts and uncles. My little sister and I only had each other. My mom was married to a man who I thought was my dad, but found out later that he was my stepdad. It never dawned on me that we had different last names until much later in life. I was a "Kelley" and my mom, stepdad, and sister were a "Dotson."

His relationship with my mom was so toxic. There was always a lot of fighting, yelling and screaming. Oftentimes, my sister and I were under the bed covering our ears to drown out the noise. We were hoping and praying that a fight did not break out. Well, one of the many times it did break out, he beat my mom and dragged her down the hall in complete chaos. My older sister tells me stories from her remembering some of the things that used to happen, but I honestly don't remember her being there. I remembering having dreams that one day he would leave and the pain would stop. He tried his best to stay, but between him, an alcoholic, and my mom, a drug user, it just didn't work and he eventually left.

Being a dark skinned, nappy head girl, and born to a drug addict mother just added to the agony. I didn't have a whole lot of friends. As it was, dark skin was not in when I was in elementary, Jr. High, and high school. And, it didn't help that the whole city knew my mom was on drugs. The pain intensified over the years and the suicidal thoughts became more of a reality to me, on a regular basis. The pain was starting to be unbearable inside and outside of my home. Outside of the home, the torture from my peers was starting to take a toll on me due to the name calling. However, the physical abuse stopped when I learned how to fight back. While I was making progress on the outside, the dark secrets started to surface on the inside. Living in a household with a drug addicted parent is not for the weak. You never know what type of day or night you are going to have; if you are going to go to bed hungry, come home to all the utilities off, or if you are going to be running from the authorities.

A lot of days, I came home to some good ole' soul food on the stove; only to be told, "It is not for you!" As the cooking ends, I wondered why I couldn't eat. Well, it was because the plates were being sold for money to buy drugs. Most nights consisted of my sister and me sitting in the closet, inches away from our mother, as she smoked her daily habit. One night, well, a lot of nights, I was awakened from my sleep to go and get in the closet. I had a front row seat on how to prepare the cans. It started with poking the holes in the can with a safety pin, sitting the ashes on top of the holes, placing the crack rock on top of the ashes, light it up from the bottom and place your mouth over the opening of the can and inhale the fumes to get high.

She would use one of two things to smoke out of, (1) an aluminum can, or (2) a piece of plastic pipe stuffed with brillo pads in one end. We were not allowed to leave the closet until about 15-20 minutes after she started because she was so paranoid. We had to sit quietly until she came down off of her high only to be back in that closet before the night was over. We had gotten so used to sitting in the closet that when we saw a paper towel balled up in her hand, my sister and I already knew what time it was. Closet time!

I also had front row closet seats to a lot of arguments and fights between my mom and her drug buddies. Who would have ever thought that the best place to be in the house was the same place I was forced to sit in? I called it my hideaway.

Eventually, I started going to my hideaway for comfort. I would sit with my crying sister until she fell asleep. I would write, hope, and pray that one day someone would come, grab my hand, and say, "I got you." That day never came.

CHAPTER TWO

I always thought that maybe one day the normal life would come creeping up on me. Maybe it would show up and completely blindside me and ask me, "Where have you been hiding?" For years, I wondered if those words – Normal Life - ever existed. What was normal? What does normal feel like? What do normal people do? I struggled with these questions for years. Again, my normal consisted of things that will have the "normal" person thinking they were abnormal. I'm often asked, "How did you manage?" I don't know how I managed, I just did. Thinking about it though, I guess the best way to answer that question is "BUT GOD."

The things that went on in my life were to be kept a secret. For a while, I thought a lot of it had to do with the shame it would bring to my family because of the position my grandmother held in the community. However, over the years, I honestly don't think it was due to anyone's position, but rather a whole lot to do with pride. I contemplated for years on not caring about anyone else's pride and getting me the help I so desperately needed. In hindsight, no one cared about my pride. I was the one being tortured night by day, sitting in that dark closet, not having any food to eat, at times not having clean clothes to wear; not knowing if I was coming or going, not having anyone to just hold my hand and say, "Baby, you are going to be okay." So, why should I care about anyone else's pride?

Well, with nowhere to go and no one to talk to I had to swallow MY pride, suck it up and just deal with it. I had to believe that one day, just one day, it would get better even if that meant I had to run until I couldn't run anymore. But, in a small city where everyone knows everyone, and my grandma, the moments when I felt like I wanted to run and get away, or run to someone for help, I was afraid. I didn't trust anyone to help me because I just knew they would go telling on me. And if running didn't work, I could always go back to "THE" definite solution that would solve it all – suicide.

So, here I was, taking care of my 8 year old sister. I'm thinking, "Why should I be responsible for her?" That's what I was thinking a lot of the time, feeling like I had no choice; it was the right thing to do. It seemed that I was the only adult in the house. From waking up in the morning to going to bed at night, I was responsible for her. I had to make sure she had something to eat whether it was a peanut butter sandwich or stealing something out of the kitchen when my mom walked away to make sure she ate. I mean, who steals from their own kitchen? It was crazy! We ate Spam or Vienna Sausages on a regular because it was the easiest to steal and eat without needing pots, pans, or the stove to cook.

I made sure my sister had clean clothes for school and her hair was done so she would not have to endure any of the cruelty from the kids at school. And, as much as possible, I kept her away from the dangers inside of the home. During the day, I didn't really focus on schoolwork, which, of course, meant bad grades and falling behind. The things that were going on were on repeat in my head. I had replayed scenarios over and over on how to escape this "normal life."

Going home had begun to feel like a death trap. But, when I went outside of the home, there was a sense of freedom. In spite of that sense of freedom, I had so much hurt and pain on the inside that I couldn't enjoy the freedom that I thought I had. At my age, I had already experienced about as much as what an adult would have experienced in a bad relationship. My heart and soul was dying because no one was to EVER know what I was enduring. I suffered being constantly hit, cursed out, and touched inappropriately by the monsters that used to hang out at my house. I was deprived of childhood things and I kept them hidden.

My friends were never allowed to come in, not that the few I had wanted to because the men that looked like giant monsters frightened them. And, one of those monsters I should have been afraid of as well. He was just that, a big ugly nasty monster. He would touch me in places that were to be touched only when I bathed and he would kiss me starting with a kiss on the forehead and eventually on my lips. I was told by the monster that if I ever told anyone he would not be happy and he would hurt me and my little sister. I believed him, so I wouldn't dare say anything. I eventually went to my mom, several times and told her that the monster was not being nice to me, even though that was his promise. I was told to shut up, stop lying and go somewhere.

Go somewhere? Like, where was I supposed to go? Who was going to help me? I went somewhere though. To my spot...my hideaway...and just sat there knees to chest and cried. When I came out of my hideaway the monster was still there laughing, talking, eating, and smoking with my mom and I couldn't understand that. And, it happened over and over again.

I often wondered that when my mom looked at me, if she could see my heart or did she just see me...flesh. After a few looks and a few more conversations about what was happening, I answered my own question. She couldn't even see my heart, soul, or my mind. All she saw was my flesh. It was then that I realized that this was a fight that I was going to have to fight alone. But, why did it have to be like this when I had a mother that was supposed to fight for me? I had to fight with all my might and that's when it hit me that I was _'Fighting to Win'._ Now, I didn't know how to pray; I didn't know how to ask God for help. Shoot, I didn't even think God would hear me because I thought I wasn't praying right. Feeling all alone, I was going to fight to win this and every battle that was thrown at me.

CHAPTER THREE

One battle that I had to conquer was this "THE" solution battle of thinking suicide was my winning ticket. When I first attempted suicide, I was 10 years old. It seemed that no one could help me and it seemed that God wasn't listening to me. So, I went to my mom's room and grabbed a clear plastic bottle off her dresser. After I opened it, I took about 10 white pills in my hand and ran to my hideaway. I cried for a few minutes apologizing to the walls around me for what I was about to do, threw my head back, and swallowed about six pills. I started to gag on the immediate sour taste in my mouth.

That scared me, so I ran into the kitchen and told my mom what I had done. She yelled for one of the people that were in the house and they grabbed me and begin forcing me to vomit. They made me rinse my mouth out with water and made me drink milk and eat several pieces of bread. This went on for about 30 minutes and eventually I started to feel better. Dizzy, but better. My mom yelled at me for about 15 minutes and made me lie down on the couch. But, she also continued to yell, curse, call me stupid, and degrade me for what I had done. Needless to say I learned that day that six aspirins will not kill you. It'll just make you very, very sick. It also will not get the police involved. They really could have helped rescue me from that place, which is what I was hoping for once I realized I had not died.

After what seemed like an eternity of the verbal abuse, I closed my heart to the hurtful words that were being thrown at me and died emotionally. I felt stupid. "How could it not work?" I asked myself. I didn't feel stupid for the attempt; it was more because it did not work. I prayed for the emotional rollercoaster I was on to stop. When mom was cursing and fussing at me, I started praying Psalms 23. At that time, that's when I thought God was listening to me because I could not hear anything else coming from my mom's lips. After the rollercoaster stopped, my mom headed to her favorite spot in the house and silence fell upon her. It wasn't due to my prayers for everything to stop it was due to her paranoia from getting high.

Across from her, in that closet, I sat thinking about how protective she was of us when she got high, but when I needed her most it was like I was her enemy. If only she could be like that full-time, protective without being high, maybe, just maybe, things would have been different. Would I have been mistreated? Would I have been touched? Would she be capable of giving me that motherly love that I needed and longed for? I couldn't understand how her motherly instincts kicked in, like a mother bear to her cub, when she was high and truly unable to care for me or protect me. Once we were released from the closet, after she came down off of her high, of course, my sister and I performed our normal routine and that was bathing, food, and bedtime. And my normal, what I knew as normal, was back.

One of the things we enjoyed doing, with little chaos, was watching TV. We had a 13" colored television that we used antenna's with aluminum foil on the ends to get the basic channels. I loved The Beverly Hillbillies show. I used to talk to Ellie May through the TV with hopes that one day she would hear me and take that same gun she used throughout the episode and come and rescue me. Ha! Needless to say, that never happened. Nonetheless, watching the show and talking to her did give me a sense of peace. I used to think, "Man how crazy is this to be sitting here talking to a character on TV and pretending she hears me?" WOW! To me, it seemed that Ellie May was fighting to win as well.

She was trying to protect what was rightfully hers and I was doing the same, fighting for my sanity, fighting for my mom's love, fighting for my sister, and fighting to protect my mind, body and soul. I didn't know how I was going to make out in this fight, but whoever challenged me needed to know it wasn't going to be easy. After the failed suicide attempt, I was determined to go in head first like a bull with sharp horns and rip apart the enemy whoever it was. After months of the abuse, physically and mentally, I had decided to stand taller than the empire state building. I figured the only way out was to use my voice that I had and not just in my hideaway. I was going to tell whoever would listen to me.

I had got word that DCF was on to my mom. I remember hearing arguments between her and, who I assumed was, my grandmother about the care that she was providing for me and my sister. It baffled me though that my grandmother had so much input, but yet my sister and I were left in the same situation. Once I learned what DCF was, the Department of Children and Family Services I thought to myself FINALLY some help is on the way. I remember getting a visit at school from a Caucasian lady, named Susan. But, prior to that meeting, I was told that I better not tell her about certain things that were going on in the house or else they would take us and place us in foster care. The horrible stories I heard about foster care where the same stories of what that ugly nasty monster did to me. Well, that scared the crap out of me!

How could I tell what was going on? Who would I be sent to? What would happen to my sister? With all the questions and fear of being in the hands on another monster, I refused to answer any questions. This lady had to be smart about her job because the look in my eyes wasn't enough to make her doubt what I was saying. That's when it hit me. She was just like my mom, looking at my flesh and not my heart, mind or soul. I didn't know any other way for this woman to get me or to get what was going on without my mom knowing I had spilled the beans. That night, I went to my hideaway and cried, rocked and again begin to pray.

This time, the prayer to God was to send someone my way that would look into my heart and my soul. It felt like God wasn't listening to me again; no one showed up. After every visit, my mom would always ask, "What did that lady say to you?" "What did you say to her?" "Did you tell her anything you were not supposed to tell?" Of course, the answer was no because I was too afraid to tell her anything based on the threats and fear of telling the truth. When I saw the caseworker my heart would smile, saying, "There is my help!" But, I couldn't, no matter how hard I tried, get the words from my soul to my lips to tell her the truth. At the end of each visit, I would just weep. I blamed myself for a long time believing it was my fault that we were still suffering and dealing with things that drove me crazy.

Here is another thing I remembered. I often noticed my mom would walk around the house bent over looking at the floor, placing her finger on the floor and then to her mouth. For a long time, I was confused as to why she did that. I would go over to the spots she had went over and look at the floor to see if I could see what she saw. Well, I never saw anything until one day I finally realized what she was doing. She was going around the floor tasting anything white or cream in color thinking it may be drugs. Some of the company she kept at our house would cut up and bag there crack cocaine and drop some crumbs on the floor. She would go behind them in hopes of finding crumbs from the cocaine when she had no money to pay for any. I learned a lesson the hard way one day. Apparently, as I was walking into the living room, I stepped on or was close to stepping on something white and she thought it was crack. I was pushed out of the way into the coffee table, almost breaking the glass, to make sure I didn't step on whatever it was on the floor. From that moment on, I was real careful where I stepped.

CHAPTER FOUR

My sister and I became very close with a young lady named Tonya. Her mom was on crack as well, so she actually understood me. You know, she got me; she knew the pain and suffering on a personal level. My mom would often hang out with her mom and they would get high together. That meant we got to spend a lot of time together. Tonya had asthma really bad. Many of nights, we would sit in my bedroom with the window open so she could get some air.

The smoke was so bad at times she could barely breathe. I would always tell her one day, my friend, one day this will all be over. Tonya, her mom, and sisters lived in a trailer park almost directly behind my house. Many times, that is the place we would go running to for shelter. Her mom was so nice to me and she was the only one, at the time, that would say to me "Del, you are one pretty lil' black girl."

I figured she had smoked so much that day it had her talking crazy. Me? Pretty? Yeah right. Black! Yep, I was that. But, pretty? I would say to myself, "Lady you are crazy!" I was probably the darkest little girl in the neighborhood with big lips, nappy hair, weighed maybe 100lbs soak and wet, wore the shoes that were called "Catheads," and half of the time my clothes were wrinkled or they didn't match. But, I was pretty? I just knew that lady was high when she talked to me. I would go home after hanging out at their house and play the words over and over in my head what she said to me. Then, I'd look at myself in that ole' faithful mirror. What I saw was a hurt, ugly person inside and out. I asked the mirror, "How can I be pretty when I have so much hurt in my heart that is seeping through my image?"

I tell you the truth, pain is ugly and some pain is unbearable. So how could I be pretty? The mirror, just like my mom, never spoke to me. It spoke at me, like my mom, by revealing the image of myself that stood in front of it. I stopped looking at myself in the mirror for a while; making a promise that I would stay away until I can see someone different. I couldn't dare keep looking at the pain in my eyes. I couldn't bear looking at total darkness from my skin color to my soul. I went back to my hideaway and thought long and hard. When I would sit in my hideaway, I felt that I was untouchable. No one could hurt me there; the hideaway never hurt me. I trusted myself in that special place. I would leave my paper and pencil in the hideaway, and no one ever found it. Everything was safe in the hideaway, my thoughts, my feelings, my emotions, my sister, and me.

Now, if I could have figured out a way to take the hideaway with me everywhere I went I think I would have been able to start living an abnormal life. Yes, abnormal to what was my normal. But, in a way, I guess you can say I took it with me because my hideaway was so dark and quiet. Even though the sun was shining bright outside, my inside was dark and quiet. The only difference is that at my hideaway, at home, no one could see me – the inner me. And, once I left the house, everyone could see – the outer me. To get to my inner layer, you had to dig deep, and I didn't allow anyone to do that. After all, why should I? In my mind, everyone was out to hurt me or make me sad. So, the best thing to do was to keep my hideaway a secret for as long as I could. The last thing I needed was for someone to figure out a way to get into my hideaway and take it away from me. What would I do if that happened? I didn't have an answer for that and until I could figure one out, I had to keep it a secret as long as I could.

The social worker from previous days was starting to come by more than before and it had started to frighten my mom. She yelled at me more thinking I had tipped the lady off. Lord knows I didn't tip her off. She started asking specific questions about the living environment, the cleanliness of the house, and the people that were hanging around the house. While still not telling it all, I was starting to think that being in my hideaway at night crying, writing, and praying was paying off. I had started to believe that I really did know how to pray all along, and that God was finally listening to me. My prayer was for myself to be patient and wait on God.

The Book of Psalms was my favorite book to read because it gave me comfort. Psalms talks about being patient and waiting on the Lord and trusting the Lord. I would read Psalms 118:8 (ESV), "It is better to take refuge in the Lord, than to trust in man." This lil' girl was growing up and I had to learn how to depend on these words to be true for me; how to trust and believe that. Because man? I didn't trust man at all! I was learning how to do Proverbs 3:5-6 (ESV), "Trust in the Lord with all your heart, and do not lean on your own understanding. In all your ways acknowledge him, and he will make straight your paths." My heart was telling me that finally God is listening.

The next time I saw the social worker I asked her, "Did God send you to me?" She never looked at my flesh again she was starting to see my heart, mind and soul. "Lord I thank you!" This is what I said every night from that point on, while in my hideaway. At last! Someone, besides the walls in my hideaway, was hearing my cries.

CHAPTER FIVE

I t took a while for the social worker to actually feel my heart, mind and soul because my life was a process. It had be to researched, dissected, and studied before you could actually understand my feelings. This is a huge relief that she was sent my way. My mom had made up in her mind that we were not going to be taken away from her, which caused for desperate measures on her part. She had begun to make it appear, from the outside looking in, that things were absolutely amazing even though they were not.

We were coming home to cooked meals after school, a clean house, not as much company and she had even started to talk to me and treat me a little different. It was almost like I had died and gone to heaven. I used to hear my elders talking about how peaceful heaven was. Well, I mentally put myself in heaven because it seemed that peace had come my way. Heaven was feeling mighty good. After all my praying and talking to God, and the walls in my hideaway, He heard me and attended to my cries, and sent me the help I yearned for. Amazingly, God had been listening the whole time. He is an awesome God and He gave me what I needed. Even though I felt like it took too long, He was on time.

For a few weeks, maybe even months, there was peace. I could finally go into that same kitchen I was told to stay away from and eat freely. I was able to sit in my living room and watch the TV, without worrying about being sent to my room because of unwanted guest that I couldn't stand to look at. I went to school with my hair combed more than usual, and had a choice of clean clothes now. My, my, my! What a feeling! Love! I had begun to feel loved, and it felt amazing. I never felt anything like it before. It felt so good I just wanted to wrap myself up in the love that was being given and never let it go. At this point, I found myself in my hideaway more than ever. The walls in there seemed like they were brighter. My heart and my soul were smiling and it showed even in that dark closet. That's what made it bright. My smile! I was starting to question myself and ask myself, "Why have I been putting myself in this closet all this time?" I just couldn't draw a clear picture of my emotions at this point. And, to tell the truth, I don't think I wanted to understand it. I didn't care about the past at the moment, but I knew I didn't want to go back to that dark place. Whatever I had to do to make sure I didn't go back there, I was willing to fight and do it.

The social worker came around a few more times. Not only was she talking with me and my sister, she started talking with my mom as well. This only went on for a few more weeks and suddenly she stopped coming by as often. I noticed it, but things were going so great in my life I didn't care so I never questioned it. Lo and behold, a week or two after her final visit that dark cloud moved back over my life. The lights started to dim on the place that was glowing like a Christmas tree. Eventually, it was getting as dark as it was before the sun started to shine through the walls. My understanding of what was going on was now at the forefront of my brain. It was all a show...................

You see, the social worker was there to make sure that mom was being the mom that she was supposed to be. She was there to make sure that my sister and I received the care that we were supposed to be receiving. Her role was to make sure that the reported rumors were not true. Just when the sun was starting to hang around, the darkness was rumbling. How could this happen to me? I'm not sure I was ever going to receive an answer to that question. But, I do know this...I was angry!

As quick as the sun left the darkness came, and I was right back at, "Who can I trust?" I know the bible talks about trusting God, but how do you do that when it seems like the same God I was praying to have left me to fight this battle again. I wouldn't dare put my trust in mom who failed me again, and yet again. How could I possibly trust that social worker who I thought was finally starting to see my heart, mind, and soul? The one who had left me there and disappeared off of the face of the earth or at least disappeared from my life so swiftly? I only trusted me. This was a hard thing to deal with. Soon, and very soon, my sister and I went back to the "Normal Life." No food, dirty clothes, house full of unruly and unwanted guest, and back to my hideaway I went to cry, write, and pray! I started asking myself, "Why pray?" I had prayed so much, and when I thought God was listening and had finally heard me I was back in my hideaway praying even harder. "Why should I have to do this?"

That answer didn't come until much later in life! The anger increased, my attitude was sharp, and my entire outlook on life was changing. I felt as if I couldn't trust anyone; as if everyone was out to get me, hurt me, or turn their back on me. For this reason or another, I just couldn't seem to figure out this this called "LIFE." As the days, and months, went by, I started to just go with the flow; convincing myself that this is it. I was doing what they call "sucking it up" and accepting the fact the things that were going on to me and around me. Learning to deal with it the best I could was the choice at this point.

As time went, I would catch myself thinking about ways to make things better. Going to tell someone else was one way. But, my thinking was that they would think I was crazy. As a young person, it's easy to think what you think other people are thinking. That's the kind of stuff that kept me in my hideaway. I had to get there to think. And, the one person that I thought saw and believed, enough to get us out of this place, was the one person who left us there. So to me, if the one person that could have made a difference turned and walked away, who else would turn and do the same? I had made up in my mind that I was the only one who could help me. Hoping for someone to show up and be what I needed was becoming hopeless. So, I started trying to help myself. I didn't know for sure how that was going to work out, but I was willing to explore different options. Heck, what did I have to lose?

CHAPTER SIX

L iving this kind of life made the days seem very short, and the nights seemed pretty long; just slowly ticking away. It was probably due to the fact that I dreaded going home. While trying to rest, I'd lay in bed trying to paint a picture of my future. I wanted to paint such a bright picture filled with love and excitement, and hoped that when I woke up I would have been placed in the center of that magical picture and started life all over again. The picture in my head was so different than the picture from my heart. The picture that my heart wanted to paint had me trapped in the middle of a dark, nasty, hell storm with no way out. It was scary. No matter how fast I ran, I couldn't escape. I kept my heart and feelings so sheltered from others that even when I thought I could run, and talk to someone, I doubted myself. A lack of trust is a terrible thing to life without.

Seconds, minutes, hours, and days had passed. After a while the social worker started coming around again. I was so emotionally consumed with my thoughts and feelings that I had buried myself inside of my own little world. The good thing is that while I was buried alive, someone was still out there watching what was going on. The caseworker had begun to chip away at me. I finally said to myself, "If you want help you have to be willing to talk and accept it." Every time she would ask me a question, I would say to her, "Let me ask you a question." And, that's how I talked to her. I would give her scenarios and ask her what she would do in this situation. If she couldn't answer me, I had already made up in my mind that I would not talk to her. But, if she was able to answer my questions I would talk to her.

After several visits to the school, and my house, I saw her finally starting to look at my heart, and not my flesh, again. This could be the beginning to me getting the help I need. Our conversations went from tell me about your day to, "Del, let me ask you something," and "I want you to be honest with me, I am here to help you." How could I not be honest with someone who was sincerely being honest with me? It would not be fair for me to not be honest with her. This time, my mom grew more and more angry and agitated. Was it because she was starting to see what I saw on a regular? Or, was it because I was letting the caseworker into our world to see what she needed to see? Either way it was pissing her off.

The caseworker didn't care. She was coming around frequently, making observations about things and developed a plan to fix it. My mom did what I knew would happen if the heat was starting to get hot and that was get us out of there. We went to Tonya's house for a few days, but this time the running was not a smart move. The caseworker along with the authorities was in hot pursuit to find us. Eventually, mom called DCF and told them where we were. They came and got us and my mom cried and begged the social worker to let us stay there. She said that she wouldn't run again. HA! And they believed her! Mom was put on a plan to get it together or there was talk about removing us from the home.

"Oh no, what did I do?" I was told several times that if I let "them people" know what was going on that they may separate my sister and I. Blaming myself for this, I wanted to fix it. Run, shut up, or keep talking? Those were my picks. If only I had kept my mouth and my heart shut this would not be going on. I was once again being blamed for something that was well out of my control. A part of me felt lost, but another part of me was relieved that someone was finally willing to take control of this situation regardless of how I felt.

Again, after several visits things seemed as if they were finally getting on track, again. Coming home to cooked food that was for me seemed too good to be true, having clean clothes for school was unreal, and finally looking like someone's child and not a throw away had me starting to believe that I was in fact what my friend's mom told me and that was that I was beautiful. I had to trick my mind into believing that I was winning this fight and the storm was finally over. I had made it through. The house felt so empty when I came home from school because the monster or the unwanted company had vanished.

The house was quiet at night. Mom still did her thing with the drugs, but it seemed as if she wasn't doing as much. My sister and I were not in her bedroom closet as much and I spent a lot of time away from my hideaway. I still went in there to write, but it seemed as though my hideaway was much brighter again. I often went into the hideaway without my pen and paper and just talked to the walls. I was so overjoyed that things finally seemed normal. You know normal that was opposite of my normal. I was now a kid at heart, mind, body, and soul. For the first time in my life, I felt as if the world was no longer on my shoulders and it was right were it needed to be and that's beneath the soles of my feet. I could talk to mom now about school and know for a fact that she was actually listening to me. She was not just looking at me she was actually hearing me. I could tell by the way she responded to me, the way she looked at me, and the way she talked with me. She went from talking at me to actually talking with me and it felt amazing.

At night my sister and I were actually allowed to help her in the kitchen to cook. It started to feel like a family. Something I had longed for, for such a long time. I used to hear my peers at school talk about the things that they did with their parents and I was so jealous because I didn't have that at home. Now, I was starting to relate to what they were talking about. The only thing that was still missing in my family was a dad. But hey, I was just so overjoyed with having what seemed like a family that I didn't care. You can't really miss something that you never had. Because I didn't know how long this was going to last, I was going to hold on to it as long as I could. I promised myself that I would hold this moment in my heart as well as in the moment.

CHAPTER SEVEN

M om seemed so different, but in a good way. The people that came around seemed to be different too, in a good way. But, for some reason, my heart just wouldn't allow me to let anyone in. The wall of my heart was so tall and strong that it was going to take a bulldozer going a 100 miles an hour to break it down. The family life went on for a few months and I loved every minute of it. I couldn't help but wonder and ponder, "Is this a dream? Was this real life? Was this "MY LIFE?"

Well, as soon as I thought this was the good life, somebody turned back the hands of time. Mom had started to back track and allow the company, as well as the monster, back into our house. My sister and I retreated to the closet again, watching her get high. The food was slowly starting to be sold again for drugs, and our living conditions had started to change again. Thank God I had my hideaway, because, once again, it was needed. It was the seatbelt on my rollercoaster. My days were starting to look dark and gloomy again and the world that was under my feet was upon my shoulders again. Often, I ran to my hideaway and cried my little heart out. "How could this be happening to me again?" I had turned another page in life and the same pattern was still there. I was so upset, angry, and hurt that I felt as if I could not cry, scream or yell anymore. My feelings, thoughts, emotions…my whole life was numb. Once again, I just knew the only way out of this was to take my own. And, over the next couple of days, I contemplated on just how to do that.

After the failed attempt with the aspirins, I had to think long and hard for a sure way to get off this ride. You know, a way that would make room for no mishaps. Then it hit me. The only way was to shoot myself. But, where the heck would I get the gun? I had to really sit back and think of a way to get one. Although guns were very hard to come by, a friend of mom's had one. But, getting it in my hands was a problem. Then, I thought about hanging myself in my hideaway. But, I did not want to hurt my sister or the walls that trusted me. The reason I figured I could get away with it there was because no one would find me right away to stop me. As I sat in my hideaway, and thought out a plan to make that happen, it seemed as if the walls spoke to me. They asked me, "How could you disappoint me and do something so drastic inside of this place so sacred to you?"

I felt that my sister would find me and she trusted me with all her heart. That was more likely to happen than anyone else finding me since she was the only person that knew of my hideaway and what it meant to me. Deadbeat tired of what I was going through, I couldn't take it anymore. I was tired of being hurt physically & mentally and I just didn't care. Over and over, I played the scenario in my head on how to get that gun I saw, how to end it in my hideaway. Even if it wasn't going to happen, which was very likely, I had to stay focused on the next plan. Finally, I had come up with a plan. Mom had a thick brown belt that she would use to beat me with. No matter how hard I held on to that belt out of all the tugging back and forth we did, that belt would not break. So, this was my plan: tie the belt around the rod in the closet to hang the clothes on and then tie it around my neck and let myself down off of the chair. I spoke with my sister and told her how much I loved her, never telling her my plan because I thought she would spill the beans. I went to school and spoke to a few peers that I semi trusted and liked and just held conversation with them about our school year together and I wished them well with their future endeavors. Not one person questioned any of it and no eyebrows were raised. I told myself that morning that this would be my last day here on earth. I had my plan, I had figured it out and I was ready to go.

After school, I went home and when I walked into the house mom was in one of her fits. The house was full of the unwanted company, so to me my decision would definitely be the right one. As the day went on I went back and forth on the "perfect time" to do it. "Should I say my final goodbye to mom?" "Should I not go through with it or what?" Well, I had decided to go ahead and do it. I went to my hideaway and prayed real hard, asking God to forgive me for what I was about to do because according to the bible suicide was a sin. But, being a kid when I read the bible, or when I heard anyone talk about God, they talked about him being a forgiving God. To me He was going to forgive me. As night fell, and mom and her friends were in a coma, I had made up in my mind the time was right.

When I had finally got my sister asleep I went into the kitchen and got a can of Vienna Sausages and some bread. I wrote my sister a note telling her that I loved her dearly and that when she woke up I would no longer be there; that I wanted her to continue to live her life no matter whatever happens to me. I knew she would be okay because her relationship with our mom was okay. It was much different from our relationship, and at the time I never knew why. She loved mom and mom loved her. I am sure my mom loved me, but their relationship was always at its best. In my note, I was leaving her the food for her breakfast. After writing the note, I leaned down and kissed her and backed into my hideaway. I cried for a while, while thinking about not doing it. The people I would hurt came rushing through my mind, even though the list only consisted of about three people. I didn't know how to separate my emotions from my desire to go ahead with my plans. Again, I apologized for what I was about to do and finally went back into the kitchen and drug a chair into my hideaway. It took me about 30 minutes to get the belt tied around the pole, as well as my neck, because my hands were shaking so bad that I could barely tie the knots.

CHAPTER EIGHT

Eventually, I got the knots tied and sat on my knees crying. Pulling myself together, I started talking about why this would be the right decision, and why I should go ahead and go through with it. Then, I got angry and started to blame myself for what was going on in my life. All the problems were because me, me, and me! As I thought about all this, all of a sudden I tilted myself to the right of my hideaway until the chair was away from my body.

Immediately, I felt a pull around my neck and I begin to choke. The belt was so tight that I couldn't even cough, and there was a lot of pressure in my head and ears. I begin to get sick to my stomach, all the while thinking to myself that this will be over in a few minutes; this will be over real soon. Crying was an option, but it was so hard to breath. Thinking, "Why is the taking so long?" it felt as if the oxygen was leaving my body so slow. The pressure in my head and ears intensified as I literally felt myself growing tired and weak. Within minutes I didn't know anything. Somewhere in my heart, I thought it was all over, but I heard mumbles and saw darkness. I could hear someone calling my name, but again total darkness. All of a sudden I felt a dull pressure and realize it was coming from my head. It felt like the pressure I had experienced earlier and I thought, "WOW! Death really hurts!"

Slowly I started to see some light and then I think I started to panic. When my eyes opened I realized that I was looking at someone. It was my sister. Now, I was really scared! "How did she make it here with me?" Well, she didn't make it with me. The stupid pole snapped. Apparently, I was over compensating, and when I passed out my full body weight caused the pole to snap and come down. Man, I didn't die. I just passed out! Being that I've never passed out before, I didn't understand what I was feeling. When you pass out you wake up with a pounding headache and that is what I was experiencing at that time.

My sister heard the crash and it scared her and that's what woke her up. She thought I was sleeping in my hideaway and when she saw the pole on top of me she decided to wake me up to inform me that the pole had fell on me. She had no clue what had just taken place. However, she did question me about why the belt was around my neck. I lied and she never questioned it again. I got up, untied the belt and attempted to put the pole back up with no success. I got my sister back in the bed comfortably and assured her I was okay. I was so okay that I went back to my hideaway and cried, cried, and cried some more. I was so hurt and too hurt to try again. "Why should I be left here on this earth to continue to suffer?" That is what my tears were saying. I just didn't understand it. I mean, I did everything right this time and death still failed me. I felt as if my whole life I would be a failure.

I couldn't get mom to stop the bad things she was doing, and I couldn't keep the monsters away, or stop them from hurting me; I couldn't stop my peers from taunting and hurting, and I couldn't even succeed at suicide. My whole life was a complete failure at this point. Since I didn't know the plan for my life, and couldn't figure it out I had decided to sit back on this ride and deal with whatever came my way. My ways hadn't worked, so for me there were no other choices. I was almost ashamed to come out of my hideaway, feeling as if everyone were pointing fingers at me and laughing. Physically I had not died, but mentally I was gone. At school the next day, I think I had zoned out because the only thing I could hear was my voice playing over and over in my head again about my plan to end my life. All day long, I thought, "Where did I go wrong?" While sitting around looking at my peers, it seemed that everyone was moving fast speed as I was moving in slow motion. My mom didn't know about this incident, so I kept it tucked way back in my brain. "Did I think of ways to make it work again?" Of course I did, but it must not have been meant to be with all these failed attempts.

After months of not meeting the expectations of the caseworker, mom had decided to get higher up involved to seek care for my sister and I. I am not sure of the process of what happened, but I do remember going into meetings with my mom, my sister, and my grandmother had gotten involved. After what seemed like months of this, it was decided that we should be removed from the home. The question was, "Where are we going?" Mom did not want us to be separated, but at the time my grandmother was unable to get us. I remember thinking after the meeting, "Will I ever see my sister again?" "How far away from this environment will I be?" Anxiety was high because I couldn't answer those questions, and it seemed that no one else could either.

Later on, there was a meeting with my mom, my grandmother, and my grandmother's sister. It had been decided that my great aunt would get us; we were going to live with her for an undetermined time. Almost immediately, we had to move. I cried and felt that I was finally going to be okay in life. At the same time, I also felt bad for my mom. She cried so badly. I was sad to see my mom cry as bad as she did. I can only imagine what she must have felt like losing her children. However, I was relieved that help had finally arrived. She explained to us that this would be a temporary living situation and as soon as she received the help that she needed she would be getting us back. I felt bad but I was also relieved that she was finally admitting that she had a problem and was willing to get some help. I thought about going back and talk to the caseworker and tell her that I was ok with how I was being treated and for her to go away.

At this point, it was out of my hands. The decision had been made. We went back home to get our stuff, and I declare we only had five minutes to get it together. The caseworker stood hovering over us as we gathered some things. She watched our every move as my mom sat quietly in her room, never once arguing the decision. This was so odd to me seeing that mom always had something to say, especially when it came to dealing with the authorities. She'd curse them, run from them, or totally disrespect them. She didn't care, and it surprised me that she was so quiet. The caseworker informed us that she was going to step outside for a few minutes and give us a little time with mom before we left. Mom explained to us that we were going to live with our maternal great aunt and uncle, and that this was only a temporary move. And, temporary had no definition. To me it really didn't matter because I was over the emotional and physical abuse.

Even though I felt bad for her, I was over the craziness in my life. I can remember while standing there listening to her, I eventually couldn't physically hear her anymore. I was actually looking forward to leaving and seeing what the future held in store for me. I was thinking to myself, like many other times, "FINALLY! The fight is over! I'm on my way to a better living environment with someone who will love me unconditionally. The only regret I had at that moment was that I could not take my secret hideaway with me and I was unsure if I would ever have one again. I never got a chance to go and talk to my hideaway walls; the walls that absorbed my secrets and my pain.

CHAPTER NINE

During the entire ride to my great aunt's house, I wrote in my journal about what I thought life was going to be like now. I hoped and prayed for a much better living environment, but again I was uncertain. After all, the person I trusted the most never gave me what I needed, so how could I trust and believe that someone else would? My aunt's house sat in the cul-de-sac near a ditch. It was not that far from my mom's house, but I was so lost in thought that it seemed like it took forever for us to get there. I remember the caseworker talking to my sister and I the whole ride trying to explain to us how much better this place would be, and why it was in our best interest that we were removed from my mom. Again, I had closed my heart off to any and everybody and I didn't care what she was saying. For me, things had to be proven.

When we arrived, my aunt and uncle were standing near the front door waiting for us. They, and the caseworker, seemed overjoyed to have us there. What I didn't understand was that everyone was excited except the two who it all really mattered to. I remember grabbing my sister by the arm and whispering to her that, "If this place is like moms, I will make sure to get us away from here." I promised myself that I would take my sister and we would run like hell! Nobody else was going to have a chance to hurt us.

Anyways, they welcomed us with open arms and it seemed that we had a safe place to call home. My aunt and uncle had 3 children, two boys and one girl. I remember looking at my cousins and thinking to myself man they look so happy. They were handsome and beautiful. It didn't take long to figure out that this house provided a happy lifestyle. Everyone welcomed us. It was kind of scary because I didn't know if this was real or what. I don't remember my older sister being there much, but she was going to eventually be living with us. I was excited about that. For so long, I wanted to be around my sister, but for some reason or another it wasn't possible until now.

The caseworker talked to my little sister and me before she left. She apologized several times for having to remove us from mom, but she didn't owe us an apology mom did. This was all her fault. All teary-eyed, she promised us that things would be okay and left us with numbers to call if for any reason we felt that we needed to call her or had any concerns.

After speaking with her she talked to my aunt and uncle for a few minutes and left them some information as well. When she walked out the door, I stood in the window and watched her walk back to the car and drive away until I couldn't see her anymore. I stood there for what seemed like an eternity. Feeling some kind a way, my throat was closing and my chest tightening up. I was scared.

The one person I had placed some trust in was gone. It was like losing two people in one day. Crying is what I wanted to do, but I had promised my sister that we would be okay; I had to remain strong for her. When I turned around my aunt and uncle were standing there still smiling and wanted to show me my room. I hesitated at first. When I walked towards them they turned and walked down the hall towards my new room. When I entered the room I was excited. It was so full of life. There were two beds with a nice comforter set, bears, dolls, toys, and warm blankets draped across the bed. I had to hold back tears from falling. I was overwhelmed from seeing the things that I was seeing. I never knew that a life like this for me ever existed. Immediately, I noticed a door in the back left corner of the room and as I was walking towards the door I was praying that when I opened the door it would be a closet. You know a place that would remind me of my hideaway; a place that I could make my hideaway. I would never turn my back on my hideaway!

At times in my life when I needed something or someone I had my hideaway and I was determined to reconnect with it. When I opened the door it was in fact a closet, but it was so full of life and full of character. It was what I have always envisioned my hideaway to be. Not a place for me to go sit in and cry, but a place that offered me a sense of peace. WOW! I found it! I was excited to know that I would still have my sister in the room with me. I could still protect her if I needed to. After taking in a few breaths to hold back my tears, I turned, closed the door, and walked back towards auntie and uncle to go and see what else the house offered. The house was a pretty nice size. There was plenty of food, plenty of furniture, and plenty of love poured throughout the house. There was a play area in the back yard for us, and the garage had the car and bicycles. There were bicycles for EVERYBODY! I mean me and my sister had a bike!

Auntie looked at me after a while and said, "It's going to be ok." Apparently, she noticed the nervousness and wanted to assure me that things were going to be alright. I smiled and walked away to go and find my sister. There she was in our new bedroom playing with the toys and the bears, and she didn't have a care about anything that was going on. She had found some toys so she was in heaven. At this point as long as my sister was right, so was I.

A few hours passed and my aunt and uncle just kind of let us get ourselves used to the house and being in a new place that they didn't bother us too much. For the first few hours we stayed in the room. After a while, my aunt came into the room and told us that it was time to get prepared for dinner. She had us go into the bathroom and wash our hands and then join the family in the kitchen area for dinner. When I came around the corner to the kitchen area my uncle was in the kitchen preparing the dinner to bring it to the table where everyone else was. The table was set with dishes and silverware, and everyone was sitting at the table.

I was confused! What was this all about? I sat in an open space and watched my aunt and uncle bring different dishes of food to the table and I never said a word. I was trying to figure out what was going on. When they finished bringing the food to the table, smiling, they asked everyone to join hands. Confused inside I finally asked, "What are we doing?" She explained to me that it was dinner time and at their house everyone ate dinner together, after prayer, at the same table, at the same time. Now I was really confused. This was so not normal me. Heck, I was fine if I got a sandwich for dinner. That was my norm. After my aunt explained to me what we were doing I was okay, but I was still shocked and confused on the inside. Hmm, so this is what a normal family does and I had missed out on this for so many years. This "new normal" was definitely going to take some getting used to.

It was amazing that as a family everyone sat at the table together. They laughed, joked, and just talked about the day's events as a whole. As for me, I was starting to get angry. For the past 12 years, I was denied this and I was upset. I'd spent my years learning not to worry about things that I could not change. I was so angry and I didn't know who to take my anger out on. After dinner, everyone helped clean the table as a family. My older cousin peeked in on me at times and asked if I needed anything. He was so nice. My youngest cousin was nicer I thought. He had such a soft voice when he spoke, and he always smiled. Every time I looked at him, he was smiling. I thought something was wrong with him, but I learned that that was just how he was.

CHAPTER TEN

That evening, my aunt came into our room and helped us prepare for bed. She laid out some nice pajamas and towels and led my sister to the bathroom for her bath. After my sister finished, she came out in the most colorful pajamas I had ever seen. She looked like a little Easter bunny, all excited about her pajamas as well. I went and showered and came out to even nicer pajamas. I didn't want to go to sleep; I wanted to stare at the pajamas all night. We were not used to that AT ALL! Throughout the first night there was not much talk from us to my new family. We were still warming up to them and our new surrounding.

My aunt asked me several times was I okay and I assured her I was. It was all just so new to me and had to sink in. I had to make sure that this was going to be my life. There was a need for me to know that I did not have to keep a bag packed and tennis shoes nearby in case I had to run. It didn't appear to be the case but the way my life had been thus far, nothing was impossible for my life. Promises of a good life before were not fulfilled, so it could happen again. Once we were ready for bed, my aunt and uncle came into the bedroom and said prayers with us. My uncle is a minister and his prayers were powerful. My aunt was so devoted to God that she was just as powerful almost shouting during the prayer. I was kneeling, but I kept peeking at her as she squeezed my hands so tight. I couldn't concentrate on my prayers because I was so drawn to her reaction to her prayers.

At the end of the prayer, they were walking out of the room and I called my aunt back and asked her to help me pray. I told her I prayed to God, but I didn't think He heard me until now. She hugged me and had me kneel back down beside the bed. She taught us the basic prayer that most kids say at night, "Now I lay me down to sleep, I pray the Lord my soul to keep. If I shall die before I wake, I pray the lord my soul to take, Amen." Once tucked in for bed she finally left the room. And that prayer was prayed every night after we prayed as a family. After laying there for a while, I couldn't sleep; I was in deep thought about what mom was doing. How was she handling the fact that her girls were no longer in her care? Did she even care? Was she bothered by any of it?

Anyway, when I checked on my sister she was sound asleep. I had decided to go sit inside the closet, my new hideaway. As I sat there, all the thoughts and emotions had built up and I finally let it all out. I placed my hand over my mouth, buried my head in between my knees, and hoped no one heard my weeping. I didn't want them to hear me, but I had to get that pressure off my chest. That night, I cried all sorts of tears. There were tears of pain and tears of relief; tears of joy and tears of sadness. Actually, I even cried because I felt bad for my mom. On overload, my head started to hurt and I prayed and asked God to make my pain go away. I whispered to the walls of my new hideaway and begged for things to remain normal in my life. So tired of the same ole ride, the pain, the running, and the hurt, I just wanted to be a new kind of normal. The life that I had experienced for the past 8-10 hours was what I longed for. Pulling myself together, I came out of the closet and went to the restroom, pretending like I had to go. What I was really doing was making sure no one heard me crying. When I went to bed, I tossed and turned all night long.

The next morning, my aunt came into the room to see if we were ready for some breakfast. I hadn't really slept that much, but I was not about to interrupt their pattern. So, I jumped up, went and brushed my teeth, washed my face, and headed to the table for family breakfast. I talked to my family a little more as the morning and day went on. Although I was still a little skeptical about letting them get too close to me, I felt that I could let my guard down a bit. Even though they were my family, I hadn't seen them or been around them too much to decide if I could trust them. They still had to earn my trust. I was not about to allow them to leave me fighting for answers again.

The days and months went on and the caseworker visited on occasions to make sure things was okay. We heard from mom, but not a lot. And, we saw her at our weekly meetings at DCF that she had to attend. I had begun to live a carefree life. None of the bad things in my life mattered anymore as I was happy. The days and nights I had conversations in my hideaway was awesome. My journal entries went from dark and full of grief to colorful and full of joy. I had even learned how to pray better. They, my prayers, had actually started to make sense, and, once again, God was listening and hearing me. Well, He was listening all the time; it just didn't seem like it all the time. I had such an indescribable feeling in my body and it felt that no one or nothing could take this away from me. Not even mom.

When I saw her on the visits I could tell she didn't want to be there, but courts made her be there. She would talk to us and ask how we were doing, but you can tell that it was just her talking from the outside. Nothing seemed to ever come from the inside of her, her heart, and I was over it. To me, it didn't matter anymore. I was done with the way she acted. Especially since I wasn't in her home anymore, and didn't have to fear what would happen to me. However, my little sister was super excited to see her regardless. She didn't see what I saw and I was okay with that being that I really didn't want her to see what I saw. She like me was a child but she was shielded from the pain so I was perfectly fine with her seeing mom as the best person on the face of the earth. Mom and I barely spoke to each other at those meetings. We interacted when we needed to through the caseworker, and we talked at each other. When it was time to go, we went our separate ways.

In the beginning, the meetings were on a weekly basis. Then, they were every other week, and eventually they faded and my mom did too. I would often hear my aunt on the phone, with who I assumed was my grandmother, talking about mom and the changes she needed to make and how she was not complying with the courts orders and all in order to get us back. I mean, how could she ever expect us back if she wasn't doing what was necessary to get us back? To tell the truth, I didn't think it mattered to her one way or the other. The anger I was experiencing was starting to go away as I realized that even with the extended help she was not doing what was required. To me she didn't care. So I didn't need to waste my energy and allow anger to linger in my head, thoughts and feeling.

Life was good now. I was at a happy place with a family that loved me more than life and didn't hurt me. Suicide was not an option anymore at this point. Shoot, I was too happy to do such a thing. And although I was feeling good about life and was being treated well, I also was spanked when I didn't follow the rules or got into trouble. These spankings were different than the beatings I used to get. I wasn't hit in such an abusive manner that I felt that I was about to die. I knew why I was being spanked, it was explained to me each time I did something wrong. I got it and it was okay.

After being in this new place for a while, I asked my aunt and uncle did they think that my sister and I would be able to go home and I think it hurt their feelings. They felt they were giving us the best care. When I asked them that, they came back with questions that would question me on whether or not we liked it there. I explained to them that I loved it there and the reason I asked was because I didn't want to go back home. We had very nice things at their house. Nice clothes and shoes; the best that they could provide and basically a stable environment that I was getting used to. Of course I wanted to stay, but based on the past I never knew if

I was going to be somewhere for good or if I would have to run again. I don't think they understood exactly everything that I had been through. To me, no one did, and until I decided to confide in them, the details, they wouldn't ever understand my thoughts and feelings.

CHAPTER ELEVEN

There were not a lot of kids in the neighborhood, so we played with our cousins a lot. I can remember going round and round the cul-de-sac riding the bikes they'd bought for us. I'd never laughed so much in my life! I was having a great time. After school, church, and on the weekends, we basically rode our bikes and played games with my cousins. One of my older cousins spent a lot of time at my grandmother's house. He loves my grandmother as if she was his mom. I used to wish I could spend just as much time there if not live. But, it wasn't possible at that time.

One day, I overheard my aunt saying to my uncle that she thought the caseworker would be coming back to talk to them about new living arrangements for us. I ran back to the room, and I bumped my arm on the wall along the way. I suspected she heard me and knew that I had heard her because she came to my room. She had no clue I was in the closet, my secret place, so she left. I was in the closet shaking, nearly in tears and I just rocked back and forth. I again felt that pressure in my chest, the lump in my throat, and my thoughts were racing at what seemed like a 100 mph. I didn't even want to try to understand what was about to happen...again. In this moment, I didn't know if I should grab my sister and run or if I should run by myself. I didn't want my aunt to know I heard her. So, after about 10 minutes I went into the bathroom as if I was there all along.

When I came out, my aunt was sitting in the den with my uncle. I went into the kitchen for a drink to see if she would say anything to me. She didn't, and the conversation between them had stopped. I pretended as if I had never heard a thing. I had to figure out on my own what was going on and what I was to do. At dinner time, I pretended that nothing was wrong. I was replaying what I had heard earlier, and I was definitely going to figure out what was going on. I barely slept that night, I even went to my aunts and uncles bedroom door that night to try and hear if they were talking about anything. NOTHING!

The next morning nothing was said so after school I asked my aunt if I could call my caseworker. She said yes but she was very hesitant about me calling her. My caseworker did not answer any of the numbers that she had left me but I did leave a message. She never called back and as the hours went by no one said anything. Later that night, I finally went to my aunt and asked could I talk to her. I explained to her that I heard the conversation between her and my uncle and I wanted to talk to them about what I heard. She didn't seem surprised at all as she looked and said, "Sure." She asked could it wait until after the dishes were done and everyone was settled for bed. Of course, I needed their undivided attention.

While my sister was prepping for bed, I went into my hideaway and pretended to be talking to them in there. I had to be comfortable saying what I had to say. It seems as if the walls spoke to me and said, "Just talk! Don't be afraid! You need answers." I prepared myself mentally for what I was going to say as well as what I was going to hear. We all sat at the table and before I could say a word my aunt started with, "Del, you know your uncle and I love you girls dearly right?"

My heart sank. I just knew whatever words that came out of her mouth from that point were going to crush me. I answered, "Yes, but just tell me what the conversation was all about." She then proceeded to say that they were excited when they got the initial call to get us and that they would not trade any of the memories we have created for anything else in the world. I sat there quietly and with a blank stare on my face just listening. Like, that was not what I wanted to hear from her. I just wanted her to get to the bottom of my issue at hand. My uncle started talking and he was in tears and he was basically saying the same thing that my aunt was saying. He also said that if they ever got a call to get us again that they would not hesitate getting us and would be there in the drop of a dime. I can remember asking him, "Will the caseworker be here to get us?" He was too emotional to answer.

By this time a river was flowing and my aunt just grabbed me, hugged, and kissed me and said, "Yes." I raised my voice and asked, "Why and where are we going?" I yelled how unfair that it was that we had to leave. Finally, someone had showered us with so much love, affection, attention, and care; they never hurt us one bit. Why would they do that to us? I was never faced with any of the trials and tribulations that I had experienced before, so I just did not understand why we had to go somewhere else. Once again, I was trying to understand the adult decisions about changes in my life that was now perfect.

My aunt let me cry and yell as I displayed my frustration. Once I calmed down, she said she wanted to talk to me about the decision but she wanted my sister to be a part of the conversation. So, I had to wait another night because my sister was asleep. That was fair, so I agreed. I also agreed not to say anything to my sister. The very least I could do was give them the respect of keeping my mouth shut and waiting. They hugged me tighter than the usual hugs and apologized and sent me to bed. I went to my room and it felt that I was walking on air. Sick to my stomach, with a pounding head ache, I felt like I was going to pass out. My comfort zone was waiting for me, so I went to my hideaway and fell on the floor. Because my aunt had taught me how to pray, I figured if I prayed hard and long enough God would hear and answer me. I was praying that when I woke the next morning my prayer for everything bad to go away, and everything good to remain normal, would be just that. Finally, someone had showered us with so much love, affection, and care. They never hurt us one bit.

CHAPTER TWELVE

The night slipped right on by as I sat in my hideaway until it was almost time to go to school. I was afraid to come out of the closet due to fear of the caseworker standing there ready to take us away. Exhausted from the hours of weeping and worrying, and no sleep, my eyes were so puffy that they were almost closed. While in the bathroom, I heard some noise coming from my aunt's room. When I went to the door to see what it was, my aunt was crying and it seemed to be harder than what I had done. She was crying and praying; asking God to give us peace and understanding of the situation. She was apologetic in the prayers as she asked God to cover us.

I ran back to my room and looked up at God. Clearly, I remembered saying, "Since my aunt and I are praying for the same thing, how can You not her our prayers and stop that caseworker from coming back and removing us?" I believed in my heart what my uncle told me about God, Jesus Christ. He told me that God was a forgiving God, and that He was an understanding God, and the He listens when we talk to Him and that He answers prayers. So, how could my prayers go unanswered? I was hopeful that the next day things would work out. There was a song that I remembered, I don't know the title of it, but the lyrics were, "I need you more, more than yesterday. I need you Lord, more than words can say. I need you more than ever before, I need you Lord; I need you Lord." I hummed that for as long as I could before dozing off and waking up to my aunt caressing my forehead. I could tell she had been crying all night as well.

Continuing with my routine, I got up and prepared myself for school. My aunt mentioned to my sister that after school she wanted to talk to us and of course my sister, being the little jolly girl she was, was like ok and went on about her business. My aunt hugged me and promised me that things would be fine and sent us to school. That day at school was bad. I was very upset and the anger that I had bottled up inside slowly surfaced that day and became an issue. I was mad with the world, didn't want to talk to anyone, and didn't want to be bothered by anyone. I just wanted the day to be over so I could get home and speak with my aunt. It seemed that everyone in school was whispering about my situation. I know they weren't, but I was so paranoid. Feeling so overwhelmed, I left school. Yep! No one gave me permission; I just left. I was going to go home, but I knew my aunt would be upset that I had left school, or skipped school, without permission. I walked through a few paths for a little while trying to figure out what to do or where to go until school was out.

So, since I hadn't seen my friend Tonya at school, I decided to go to her house assuming she was at home. I knew they wouldn't tell on me and would allow me to be there for a little while. Plus, I figured she would be glad to see me being that we hadn't seen each other since we had moved. There was a path my mom used take us through when we were on the run sometimes. It was out of the view of anyone seeing us. When I got to her trailer park, I saw a cop car pulling into the entrance. I hid behind a trailer until he passed me and once he was out of my sight I kept going. Just before coming out of the woods to their trailer, that cop car that I had seen was at their house. I froze and ducked down into the bushes and waited for them to leave.

The cop never went inside. He just stood at the door and talked to Ms. Dot, Tonya's mom. I did see Tonya peek her head out though. After speaking to them for a few minutes, and taking notes, he handed her something and walked back to his car. He did not leave immediately he was there for a while before he pulled off. Wanting to make sure that he was gone, I waited for a few minutes before I went up to their door. Once I felt safe, I sprinted like a jaguar after its prey. I knocked on the door so hard and long that Ms. Dot was yelling. As soon as she opened the door I made a beeline inside. She was shock to see me. She immediately asked me, "What have you done?" And, I said nothing. She informed me that the police had just left her house looking for me.

I was stunned! I mean, how did they know I was heading there? She said to me that the cop said he was there to see if I had come to her house. The people at school had called my aunt when I didn't show up for my class. And, apparently, someone had seen me walking off the campus. They notified my aunt, DCF, and my mom and started to look for me. I knew then that my mom had told them there was a possibility that I would go there. I looked at Ms. Dot and I pleaded with her not to call the officer back out. I told her that I just needed to stay there for a few minutes and try and clear my head; to try and make sense of everything that was going on. She was disappointed in me that I had come to her house the way I did, but she had no idea on what was going on.

Ms. Dot was under the impression that we were fine, based on what my mom told her. She had no idea that we didn't live with mom anymore. I sat and talked with her about what had happened over the past few months. To me, she seemed to be completely surprised. Although I knew I couldn't stay there with her forever, I just needed to stay there for a few hours for my own sanity. I'm sure my aunt and uncle were worried about me, but none of that mattered to me at the time including the consequences of me running or whatever. I went in the room with Tonya and watched TV with her and played with her toys. She kept asking me questions, but I didn't have all the answers so I just cried.

I can remember telling her I don't know any more I just don't. She gave me a hug and said I would be fine. However, I started getting angry inside all over again. To me, it wasn't and I was sick of people telling me that it was. The caseworker told me that it would be okay, my aunt and uncle told me that things would be okay; now I had my friend and her mom telling that things would be okay and to me all of them were lying. It seemed that everyone was lying to me. Once again, things in my life were about to be shaken up. Ms. Dot peeked in on us, on occasions. She looked sad and confused about my situation and really couldn't help me. I stayed there for a few more hours and then I decided that I should leave so that I didn't get caught there and got Ms. Dot into trouble. Before I left, Ms. Dot made sure I had eaten something and she talked to me more about the situation. I left and went through the same path that I came. Ms. Dot told me to make sure that I go straight home. Of course, in my head, that was not the plan. But, I decided it would be best for me to go straight home. On the walk back to my aunt's house, I saw several police cars and my heart skipped a beat thinking they were looking for me.

Not wanting to take any chances, I found a few back paths back to her house. When I arrived there was a car there that I didn't recognize. I was nervous about going to the door, but it was getting late and I didn't want to continue to put them through the stress of me running away. I went to the door and rung the bell. My aunt came to the door in a rush and when she saw me she just grabbed me and hugged me. I remember her yelling out "She's back, she came back!? She cried and hugged me tight, and he came scurrying around the corner along with my caseworker. She was in a different car that's why I didn't recognize it. The three of them approached me and begin looking at me. They were turning me looking at my body, my clothes, and asking me questions making sure I wasn't hurt. They were scared and relieved at the same time. I assured them that I was okay and at first it was like no one believed me. Eventually they did and calmed down a little.

CHAPTER THIRTEEN

I saw my cousins and my sister peer their heads around the corner. My aunt grabbed my hand and we went to the kitchen table. I sat in a chair across from my aunt and uncle and the caseworker sat directly next to me. She had a folder with her and she opened it and she had papers with her. She pulled out her cell phone and made a call to the non-emergency number to the police department. I heard her ask the person on the other end of the line if they could send an officer back out to my aunt's house. I panicked and my inner soul told me to run, but I knew I would not be fast enough to get away from them. I started shaking and she grabbed my hand gently and said not to worry, she had to call them back out because I had been reported as a missing person and he needed to come out to make sure I was okay and close the case.

I felt a little relieved, but I honestly thought she was lying to me. Everything else she had said to me I was starting to feel was a lie, even when something good happened it didn't stay good. So, trusting her was hard. She explained to me how everyone felt scared, worried, hurt, and could not process their thoughts knowing I had ran away. I said to her now you guys see how I feel. My whole life I have felt this way and when I express my feelings to no one seems to care. I started crying and yelling that I am sick of everyone around me only concerned with their feelings and no one concerned about my feelings. I told them that I was sick of holding my thoughts and concerns in and when I did let them out, because I was a child, no one heard me.

Well tonight was going to be the night that someone heard me. I told them that I thought my sister and I should be a part of every decision that was made because it was our life and we had to live it and deal with whatever they had decided for us and it wasn't fair. I told them that I felt that they treated me like a "thing" and not a person. When they spoke to me they spoke at me, no one sat down and spoke to my heart about my feelings and concerns and I was sick of it. I was going on and on and before I knew it, I yelled out that I was going to kill myself and get away from everyone and they would not have to worry about me. Immediately the room went silent for a few minutes and everyone looked around at each other. Was I serious this time? Yes and no. I hadn't made another plan to attempt suicide because things were going so well. But still, it was an option.

The doorbell rang and my aunt excused herself and came back to the kitchen with the cop following her. The caseworker caught him up to speed about what was going on and then she mentioned to him that I said I was going to kill myself. Now I was really angry with her! Once again, my personal thoughts and feelings were overlooked. The cop started to question me about the events earlier in the day and asked me questions like why I ran, where had I gone, who was I with, did I do any drugs, and was I hurt. Of course he was not going to get out of me who I was with. I responded to him by saying I was alone, no I wasn't hurt, no I didn't do any drugs, but I'm sorry sir I can't tell you where I went. It is my secret place and NO ONE will ever know where that was and I meant it. It was my right not to tell him and I wasn't. Then, he asked me about me wanting to hurt myself. I told him that I just said that because I was angry. He said that I shouldn't do that because it could cause more trouble.

It was explained to me that he could have me removed and sent to a facility where they would keep me for a few days until they decide if I was safe. I almost considered that because I felt that the people there would treat me better. He explained to me that they would not treat me any different, but they would make sure I couldn't hurt myself. That changed my mind because I didn't want to be protected from hurting myself. That wasn't the case this time. I wanted to be protected from everyone hurting me. He said that I should not run either because that could also cause trouble. After I answered his questions, I had mentally blocked him out. I went silent and never said another word to him until he made me mad. I could see he was getting angry, but I didn't even care as I sat and stared at him like he was crazy. He eventually stopped talking and began to talk to my aunt, uncle, and the caseworker. He told them that if I was to leave again for them to call and an officer would be back out.

Again, he started saying to me that if I was to leave again that I could get into trouble. And again, I didn't care what he was saying I just wanted him to shut up and leave already. He then said to me that if I was to leave again, and if I went to someone's house and they found out I was there, I could get that person into trouble. I then had something to say to him, I said to him "Good luck with that sir. You will never find out!" I was sick of him talking to me just like I was sick of everyone else. As they all talked around me, I turned away from them and stared at the floor. I asked if I could be excused and the caseworker said she wanted to talk to my sister and I about what was going on after the cop left. I was forced to sit there while they talked about me, around me. Finally her business was squared away with the cop and he left. I was sent to get my sister so that we could talk about our next step. She started off by saying that mom had went before a judge and it was decided that it would be in our best interest if we were placed to live with my grandmother or someone else.

It was also decided that it would be in mom's best interest to go away to a treatment facility and get the help that she needed. Actually, mom had agreed to go to an inpatient treatment facility in Miami, Florida. Miami is about 2 ½-3 hours away from where we lived in Cocoa, Florida. I was happy that mom realized that she could not do it on her own. Now, why so far away kind of blew me away because that meant that we could not see her anytime we were ready and I wasn't sure anyone could take us there. Nonetheless, I was ready for her to get the help she needed whether she wanted to or not. Maybe one day we could finally be a family again, if she would get herself clean. After being told that it was in our best interest to go live with our grandmother, I felt some kind of crazy for running away. We were going to be with our oldest sister. I had no clue that they were trying to place all three of us under the same roof.

I asked, "Why didn't that happen from the beginning?" I was happy where I was at and I didn't want change again.

My thinking was, "Why couldn't my older sister come and stay with us?" Not all change was for the better but obviously others thought differently. The courts had actually listened to mom since she had decided to get help, this was her choice and everyone, except the kids, agreed. Seemingly, as always, our opinions about the matter didn't matter. Another question I had was, "How soon was this move for mom, and how soon the move was for us?" The caseworker explained to me that the move for us was going to happen in about two weeks. The courts had the final say and they had to get everything regarding mom's treatment finalized. They were waiting on an approved spot to open up in the program that was working to get her help.

CHAPTER FOURTEEN

Going to my grandmother's house to be with my sister and other close relatives seemed like a great idea, so I didn't really understand why I allowed myself to get so upset. I think my aunt was so upset because I was. The truth is that I didn't like the fact that we had to move again, especially leaving my aunt and uncle. However, if I could be with my sisters and my immediate aunts and uncles, I was okay with that. The caseworker let us know that we were still considered to be under state care and have to talk to her on occasions until my grandmother received the final custody paperwork.

Being under state care comes with strict rules especially when it came to our whereabouts. It sounded to me that we would live like we were outside prisoners. You know, locked up without being behind bars. I would still be controlled by the state. They had to know our every move. We would not be allowed to be around certain people or go certain places. This was just too much to deal with as a 12 year old. I had been faced with so many adults choices and decisions that my mind was on overload. Not knowing how to process all these decisions and changes, I needed space to clear my racing mind, so I asked was there anything else we needed to talk about after getting something to eat, I was ready to go to bed. This time though, things were much different. After my shower and prayers with my aunt, I waited until I heard her door shut and I went into my hideaway.

Confused about a lot of what I was told, I couldn't even gather my thoughts to try and figure out anything. All cried out, I honestly couldn't cry anymore; so I THOUGHT. I was so ready for this way of living to finally be over...calm...settled once and for all. It was a done deal; we were going to live with my grandmother and my sister. The only thing I was concerned with was finding a new hideaway. There were so many unknown things like, would I have my privacy or find another hideaway. It scared me that I didn't know what the environment or living arrangements would be like on the inside. I needed to know that. Although I was unclear of everything happening, I prayed and smiled that night in my hideaway. My mom was getting help and my sisters and I were finally going to be together.

Over the next few days, we (my auntie, uncle, and my cousins) laughed, cried, talked, and prayed together. They promised me that they were just a phone call away and anytime I wanted to see them all I had to do was call. I believed them and the anger I was feeling the night before was gone. It wasn't their fault that we had to leave and I had to realize that. After a few more days, we didn't talk about the leave anymore. Even though it was an okay decision, it still hurt to leave a family that had devoted so much love, time, attention and affection to me and my sister. I know they were my family, but it was still hard to leave. When the time came to pack, I didn't come with much so I didn't have a whole lot to leave with. My aunt let me take a few things with me to my granny's house. Everything else, she kept, so if we ever needed to come back we would have it. I was okay with that. I was hoping she would keep some memories of me!

The caseworker was fully responsible for our transition and she had to sign off that she picked us up and got us to our grandmother's house. That was another one of the state's requirements. It was ridiculous if you ask me, but they make the rules and their people follow them. I hadn't seen mom over the two week period and I'm not sure where she was at. Although I wondered where she was, I didn't ask anyone and no one mentioned her at all during the time. We got to my grandmother's house and everyone was excited to see us and I was excited to see my older sister. The caseworker was talking to my grandmother and she was giving her all kinds of documents. I wasn't really paying attention to any of it, because I immediately begin to focus on where I would sleep. My main concern was finding me my own secret hideaway.

We were showed our bedroom and because my grandmother's house was not that big, and several people lived there, the three of us had to share a room. And guess what? There was NO hideaway. There was a closet, but it was a long closet that held my grandmothers sewing machine and a lot of other items as well as our clothes. It wasn't private at all. I felt like I was going to pass out. Where was I going to go to get away; to write, to pray, to cry, and to talk? I didn't like this not one bit. I didn't have a choice in the matter at all and wanted to run as far as I could. Soon as there was something I didn't like, I was ready to run. Maybe I could go back to my aunt's house? I had to find a hideaway because it was the only thing that kept me calm at times. My hideaway was my only friend; my safe haven. I couldn't stay there.

We walked back to the front of the house and the caseworker was finishing up with my grandmother. I asked her could I talk to her before she left, but I didn't want anyone to hear what I had to say. Once she finalized everything with my grandmother, I followed her outside. I asked her could I go back to my aunt's house and she asked me why? I couldn't tell her the real reason why I wanted to go back there. My hideaway was my little secret and I was starting to lose trust in her. My excuse was that I just needed to go back to my aunt's house. I told her my aunt needed me and that she could not leave me there. Tears welled up in my eyes and she had to clear her throat and fight back tears as she explained to me that she had to leave me there and I would be okay. I told her I didn't want to keep hearing that I would be okay; I just needed to go back to my aunt's house. It hurt her to have to tell me no, but she had to leave me with my grandmother. She walked me back inside and told me she would see us later that week. I was devastated!

CHAPTER FIFTEEN

I felt that, once again, someone had failed me and this time it was the caseworker. She was the only other one, outside of my aunt and uncle, that I had trusted and I was starting to lose trust in her. The caseworker eventually left us for the day and reality set in that this was my new home. I should be happy, right? I had my granny, my sister, and my aunts and uncles, but I still felt empty? Although I was young, I was becoming mature for my age. And, I was tired of trying to get to know new people and trying to figure out who was going to be there for me and not hurt me. I didn't want to keep going through that.

As night fell, all I could think about was where in the house I could go to write, cry and pray. My grandmother was trying to make things as normal as possible for us. It was scary being in a new place, new environment. The question to all this was, "Am I going to be able to adapt?" I think that being with my aunt and actually being loved by good people made me wonder if there were other good people to do what she did for us. What hurt me the most was that my aunt was not there to help me pray, I was crushed. I didn't think I could do that without her and I didn't think that God would hear me without her. Now that I'm grown, I know that God does hear me without other people praying for me. But as a child, I just didn't see how this was going to work. It was time for me to buckle up and ride this new ride.

Things appeared to be somewhat normal at my granny's house. The rehab facility had finally accepted my mom, and she was preparing to leave. It was an inpatient facility, which means she will have to live there. Of course, I have all sorts of questions again, "How long will she be there? Will we be able to go see her?" I had hoped we could see her and I didn't want her gone long, but I desperately wanted her to get help. Even if that meant we could not see her. I was hoping and praying that the next time we saw her she would be a different person and we could go back home. That's what I really wanted. Nonetheless, I had to be honest with myself and answer those questions truthfully. The answers that were in my heart were no. From the past hurt, pain and experiences there was no way I could answer those questions with a 100% yes and yes that things would be different. I desperately wanted, and needed, to be proven wrong. While my nights ran with my days, I often caught myself at school thinking and wondering how mom was doing. I wondered if she was being honest about her life, and about the things that involved us. I didn't quite understand, at that time, what all that going to rehab meant other than help her with the drug use.

Sleep escaped me a lot of nights. There was a constant fear that if I closed my eyes I would open them to the caseworker coming to take us somewhere else. Mostly, I was afraid because my safe place was not available to me. During the times I wasn't worried about other things, I worked on figuring out a new hideaway spot. It was the only place that I felt God actually listened to me. It was hard fallen asleep because sometimes I would have nightmares about my life. My dreams were never sweet innocent dreams; they were terrifying. I couldn't control the dreams and in the dreams, I couldn't control what was happening to me. Countless nights, I sat up or just laid there and silently cried. Sometimes, I'd go to the bathroom, several times during the night, flushing the toilet to drown out my weeping. I was hurt, distressed, and I was lost. I could not figure out for the life of me why no one understood that I was the one that was hurting and I was hurting deep down to the depths of my soul. Although I prayed for guidance and healing the best that I could, my soul was lost. I was always told to just talk to

God; that He listens. My aunt taught me John 3:16 "For God so loved the world, that he gave his only begotten son that whosoever believed in him, shall not perish but have everlasting life." She reminded me that God would never leave me nor forsake me, so I had to just trust and believe in His words. It was hard, but I had to believe.

In the midst of everything, it seemed that life was finally starting to become brighter for us. I'd finally calmed down enough, emotionally, to accept how things were with our new living arrangements and with mom. I was enrolled in the middle school near my grandmother's house. Even though I was living with my grandmother now, I was still amongst the same peers from when I lived with mom and my aunt. They were the same kids, just a year or two older, but the same exact individuals that were cruel to me a few years back. I didn't care anymore though. My pain scale was well past hurt of all hurt, so nothing they did or said bothered me that much anymore. There were a few young ladies that I had become friends with and they seemed pretty cool to hang with, so I let my guard down just a tad bit and attempted to let them in.

It took a while and it was definitely nothing easy to do, but in order to heal myself from the inside out I had to allow people in. I had to realize that I was holding myself hostage to what could very well be good people in my life. I had become very close to a few ladies: Hatasha, Latonya, Amanda, and Janise. Hatasha, Amanda and Janise had what I had longed for, and for a very long time. Their parents were still together. They had a family bond that was unbreakable to their parents especially their moms and I desired that my entire life. I was a bit jealous to know that they all lived normal lives. Latonya's situation was a lot like mine. She lived with her paternal grandmother, whereas I lived with my maternal grandmother. She had lived with her grandmother since she was a baby, so the bond between them was unbreakable as well.

You could see the love and commitment between the two of them…I wanted that so badly. So, the plan was to do what I needed to do to become friends with them and they could share some of their love and affection with me. We would talk at times about our family situation, but Hatasha, Amanda and Janise never understood exactly what I went through. I didn't expect them to because they had no experience at all. When they asked about my mom and dad, I could answer questions about my mom but not my dad. Latonya somewhat understood because she was being raised by her grandmother too. Since I considered them to be my friends, it was okay for me to share this information with them. I wanted them to understand me and know me without me telling them that I was broken deep down inside. I needed them to love me as their friend and not care or judge me, or my life and my secrets.

They did just that…love me as I was. They embraced me with open arms and I could breathe. Finally, I had someone who listened to me and cared enough for me to say to me, "Del, I'm sorry you are going through this, but you will be okay." I heard this from my friend's mouths and their hearts. I was beginning to feel like a human being and it felt good.

CHAPTER SIXTEEN

Throughout the school year, I had made some really good friends. There was another girl that I had met who was very mean to me and I hadn't done anything to her for her to treat me that way. From time to time, I would tell my teachers that she was bothering me and they would speak to her. It would stop for a few days and eventually she would go back to bothering me. Once, if not more than once, I'd threatened to beat her up if she didn't leave me alone.

However, I knew if I was suspended from school for fighting that my grandmother would let me have it so I backed down. She took my backing down as me being a coward, but that wasn't the case. I was more afraid of what would happen when I got home. One day, I told her that if she kept it up I was going to make sure that she would never be in a position to hurt me again and I meant it. Evil had got a hold of me, and I had envisioned some ways to hurt her. I didn't want to do that, but I was all about protecting myself even if that meant I had to take all of my anger out on her. From my overall friendship with Hatasha, Amanda, Janise, and Latonya I was happy, even though I kept in mind ways to hurt the bully if she didn't back down and leave me alone. Other than that, I looked forward to school every day. When the weekend rolled around, I would only see Hatasha and Latonya, but I had gotten so used to our little *"Circle of Five"* that I was able to sleep all night and look forward to Monday morning.

My grandmother had a rule in her house about sleeping in all morning and attending church on Sundays. I noticed her rules, but I was so happy that I had finally found some friends that I didn't notice that my grandmother's rules went from being rules to demands. I had become so wrapped up with the happiness from my friends that I didn't realize that my grandmother was really strict. In all actuality, she was mean. Her demeanor of being happy to get custody of us went from being warm and welcoming to almost the environment that I was familiar with growing up. She yelled and cursed; demanded things and screamed at me, at times, when she wanted something done. I didn't know how to take this.

Not too long after being there, it went from being treated like a little lost girl that someone was trying to protect to being treated like I was in reformatory school. It knocked me back and I didn't know how to deal with that. It was a déjà vu moment. The yelling, the cursing, the spankings and the meanness were alive again in my life. I asked myself, "How the heck is this possible?" On school days, we were awakened two hours early to clean the same house that we had cleaned the night before. That made no sense! If I had cleaned before bed, why should I be awakened to clean again before school especially when everyone slept at night? I was yelled at if things were not done in a certain manner.

After school, once again, yep, once again, we had to clean the house. What bothered me was that people were at the house throughout the day that messed it up and I had to come behind them and clean it. We were not allowed to go to anyone's house and we were not allowed to have any company not that anyone really wanted to come over. They all complained that my grandmother was mean. When I used to hear that, I would think that they were crazy. They were not crazy. I eventually had a run in with that mean person.

On Sundays, we were in church just about all day. We attended a church called The Salvation Healing and Miracle Center and the pastor was a lady named Dr. Lurline Smith. She was amazing and she such a sweet person. The most amazing part about this church was that it was real family oriented. Her daughters and grandchildren attended the church. Just about the whole family attended the church. Her husband was simply amazing. I would tell my sisters he is the cutest old man that I have ever seen who could sing his butt off. In fact the whole family could sing. My whole family went to the church including my aunt and uncle. Pastor Smith had two daughters that I loved to hear sing, Ms. Angela and Ms. Polly. Regardless of what I was feeling or what had happened to me throughout the week, I looked forward to Sunday morning to hear them sing. Ms. Angela used to sing a song that would always melt my heart. It was called, "Now behold the Lamb." I would tear up so bad whenever she sang, but especially when she sang that song. I can remember joining the choir and I didn't want to because I cannot sing a lick, but my grandmother forced me to.

There was a song the choir used to sand, "Hallelujah is the Highest Praise." Ms. Angela was standing next to me barely uttering a word, but my ears and heart was wide open to hear the melodies flow from her mouth. Her voice was beautiful. Ms. Angela was also the choir director and I know when we had choir rehearsal she heard my voice and probably thought "what in the world, why is she in this choir singing like that." I looked forward to Sunday mornings because I could escape the wrath of my grandmother. When I stepped foot inside of that church, I was in a carefree zone.

Some of the sermons seemed that they were directed straight to me and it seemed that Pastor Smith always looked at me when she preached. She used to call for alter prayer and when she got to me she prayed real hard over my life and she would squeeze my hand and just pray for me. I CRIED EVERYTIME. I knew God was speaking to me through her and I was listening. He told her to tell me all the time, "Del you are going to be okay, keep believing and have faith." I had to find a way to just trust that those words were the truth. They were coming from someone who never had to fight for my acceptance. After church, even though I felt I was being mistreated, my soul was at peace.

In the near long run, the physical abuse started. It was always there; it was just a matter of time before it came out. I used to say that the lady that I knew as my grandmother was mean spirited. I was right. My days and nights at her house were hurtful. I was yelled at for the smallest things from not coming fast enough when she called me to just simply sitting down watching TV when she felt we should have been cleaning, even though the house was spotless, I was hit, screamed at, called names, and treated like I was someone from the streets. I was called ugly and stupid, and was told that I was dumb. There were good days, but my bad days outweighed the good one. Since I didn't have a private hideaway, I started looking forward to my new public hideaways, school and church. They were places I felt safe; places she couldn't hurt me at. She wouldn't dare show out on me in public because she had an image to maintain. I had to live with her, so there was no way I could expose her. I was terrified of what could or would happen to me if I said anything.

CHAPTER SEVENTEEN

When the caseworker came by to visit us, I never said anything about how my grandmother was treating us. I hated the situation, but I didn't want to get my grandmother into trouble, or cause any more trouble in my life. My grandmother dated this guy and they had decided to take us down to Miami on the weekends to see mom. She was so excited to see us. The sad part was that I was happy to see her too, but I never felt a bond with her like my other sisters did, especially the baby girl. I was amazed because mom looked so different...she looked so good. Her going to this rehab was a good thing and it showed in her face and her personality.

While I was happy for her, I still tried to dig deep down in my soul and change my feelings towards her and it wasn't working. The disconnect between the two of us was so bad that even with her doing what she needed to do it was really hard for my feelings for her to change. I noticed how we were towards each other. She spoke to me when we were there, she hugged me while we were there and she even showed me off to her housemates while we were there, but there were no feelings behind it. It was different than what she did to my sisters. To me, it was the same emotions she showed me when I lived with her, empty. I just went along with the flow while we were there. The visits continued throughout her stay and then time came for her discharge. We had to have meetings with the caseworker to discuss a plan for us to either return to mom when she was discharged or stay with my grandmother or foster care. My mom and grandmother collectively decided that my grandmother would keep us if mom could not get us back. Foster care was not an option for them.

Due to the way my grandmother was treating me, I was ready to leave, but at the same time I didn't quite trust that mom would be able to take care of me. I was hoping and praying that she would and it was only fair that I gave her a chance. For a few more months, mom had remained at the facility and they were considering letting us all live with mom once she was home and settled. Throughout the remainder of mom's rehab, we had to have weekly family meetings. The meetings continued until mom was discharged and it had been decided that my older sister was going to remain with my grandmother.

Before mom came home, my little sister and I had started to spend more time with our dad. My paternal aunt would pick us up and take us to her house and also to Daytona, FL to see our grandmother and grandfather. Even though my maternal grandmother allowed us to go visit, she had strict rules as to when we were to be returned home. I was confused about the animosity between the two families because from what I can remember, my dad's family was there when I was growing up. So, I did not understand why my grandmother was so bitter. The arguments got worse over time and I was no longer allowed to go as much as my baby sister was. Again, I was confused. "Why couldn't I go?" I begin to question that and that's when I found out that my sister's dad was not my real father and the family that I knew as my aunts and uncles was a big lie. I found this out through an argument my grandmother was having on the phone. I remember her yelling, "Delatron will not be going anywhere with you all, only little sister." I asked her why I couldn't go and I was told to go sit down somewhere. What had I done? I went back in my mind trying to figure out what I had done and could not come up with anything.

Man, I needed to talk to someone. Who was I to talk to? I was wrecking my brain trying to figure out what was going on. That whole day, my grandmother was back and forth on the phone yelling and cursing and for a long time I didn't know who was on the other end. Finally, it was revealed by accident that she was arguing with my dad and his family. Then it came out that I couldn't go anymore because I was being kept away from them and because the man that I thought was my father was not my real father. The conversation was, "I have legal custody of them and I make the decisions on where they can and cannot go. Delatron Kelley will not be leaving this house with anyone. Go to the courts! Because you or nobody else don't have a say so when it comes to Delatron!" I went into the bathroom repeating what I heard trying to convince myself that what I heard was a lie. It felt like an elephant had sat on my chest; I couldn't breathe. I couldn't think! I felt sick to my stomach and I faint. I flushed the toilet a few times and turned the water on in the sink to drown out my sobs. Here I go again, pulling myself together to deal with another adult problem.

How was I going to approach this? I knew if I had said something to my grandmother I would be in trouble and be accused of listening in on her conversation and I would be punished. That was not the case, but I heard what I heard and I was extremely hurt. I was dying on the inside and I could not say one word. Then it dawned on me, this explains the difference in the last names. As painful as it was the pieces of the puzzle was coming together. Now, I wanted to find out who Delatron Kelley was. I left the bathroom and went to my room. My grandmother called for me and my heart stopped. I had a lump in my throat thinking she knew I had heard and she knew I had been crying. I answered and went to her room and she sent me to get her a glass of water. When I returned to the room with the water she said thank you and sent me on my way. WHAT THE WHAT? She had nothing to say? She didn't talk to me about anything! I could not believe that.

After I left her room my soul died. My brain was electrocuted with thoughts, "this is my fault; I'm guilty for hearing what I heard." How am I, as a child living in such a volatile situation, to approach and ask about what I was processing in my head? I just wanted out and away from everything and everyone and this time for good. That night was a good night to attempt suicide again. I went into my room and immediately my sister joined me. I ran ideas over and over in my head. I needed a way to handle my business without anyone seeing me and I needed to know how to do it to make it work. The last few attempts had failed and I was out of ideas and nowhere in the house to go and be alone.

CHAPTER EIGHTEEN

I went and showered and while I was in the shower I just cried. I wanted to know why no one had told me the truth about my father. Why did I have to find out this way? Why was it such a big secret? WHY? WHY? WHY? Better yet who is Delatron Kelley? It hurt me more to find out the way I did than them just being honest with me from the beginning. Now that I know, I also wanted to know him. No one said a word to me concerning this and I didn't expect them to. The next morning I was silent as a mouse. Barely saying anything, no one questioned why I was so separated from them that morning. Things were just as normal as they were days before.

I met up with my friends at school and they informed me that tryouts for basketball were going on and asked was I going to try out for the team. I wanted to because I wanted to be with my friends and I wanted to get away from that house. I wanted to stay with my friends and do what they were doing, but I also wanted to run away and seek answers for myself. I knew if I ran I probably would not be able to try out for the team and I didn't want to lose the friends that I had or let them down. Barely able to pay attention, I did the right thing and stayed in school that day. All day long, I kept going over scenarios of how I could talk to my grandmother, but she had put so much fear in my heart all the ways I thought of were crushed. On the way home from school, I had hyped myself up saying that I was just going to walk into her room and ask her about the phone call. Well, that hype was brought down real low because the way she called my name when I walked into the house scared that thought right out of my head.

She was yelling and screaming for me to hang some clothes out on the line. There was a list of other demands that I said, "Forget it!" I hung out the clothes and talked to God. I said to God that my aunt told me that if I just talked from my heart that He would be listening. I did that, I asked God, "Why was my life going the way that it was going?" I asked, "What had I done to deserve this lifestyle and treatment?" I questioned who I really was. My whole life to me seemed to be a big lie, a big secret I was alive physically, but what did that mean? I asked God why my biological father was kept a secret from me and why was I born into a family that would make me endure so much heartache and pain? I wiped away my tears as fast as they fell in case my grandmother or someone came out while I was hanging the clothes. I couldn't let them see me like this; it was not okay for me to cry. From the looks of things, it was apparent that I was expected not to feel any pain.

Anyways, after I finished talking and praying, I swear I heard God talk back to me and the only words I heard was "Trust Me!" It kind of scared me because everyone else always told me to trust them. Trust them things would get better, trust them that I would be okay. I didn't believe them, so why should I believe God? That's when I remembered what my aunt had said to me one night while we were praying. She said for me to always remember Proverbs 3:5, "Trust in the lord with all your heart, and do not lean on your own understanding." As a child I didn't quite understand that meaning, but later in life I knew and understand exactly what that scripture meant. I finished the laundry, pulled myself together and went inside. A few hours later, the doorbell rang and it was the caseworker. I wanted to just buckle and cry. I wanted to let her in on the conversation that I had overheard and I wanted to let her know how my grandmother's attitude had changed over the months. I was not able to do that because at this point I didn't trust her anymore.

I didn't understand how she didn't see the hurt or despair in my face that day I told her "my aunt needs me." I think people need to trust the instincts of children's sometimes? I didn't really believe anything else that she said especially after she had removed us from my aunt and placed us with my grandmother. The happy life that she had promised me was nothing near happy. The people that were in my life, and were supposed to love me and not disappoint or hurt me, were doing the total opposite. I wanted to be left alone. Shoot, I was already alone in the world, so if everyone around me disappeared I was okay with that. She talked to us for a little while then she spoke with my grandmother. Of course my grandmother didn't mention the conversation about my dad, and she certainly didn't mention the treatment that she was dishing out. From her mouth to the caseworker's ears everything was on the up-and-up. Should I say something or should I keep quite? That is the decision I was contemplating. I decided to keep quite and see how long the game would continue. I finally got Susan, the case manager. She was there for a paycheck. She wasn't there to help me. If she was, she would have seen through the B.S. with my mom, grandmother, and everyone around me and got me the heck out of there.

In my head it made sense to me why I was treated so different. The man that I knew as my father was not my father and everyone had to play the cover up game since my life, as I knew it, was a fairytale. It even turns up, amongst all the other drama, that the girl who continued to bully me actually had a connection to me. The sad part about the connection is that everyone, except me, knew and they knew why she kept bothering me. My life at this point was like a game. I was a joke to everyone except myself. Well, what no one knew was that I had had enough of their games. I decided I wasn't going to play their games or laugh at their jokes. I was going to find some peace and sanity for myself. I was done being nice!

Were they ready for my fight, my games, and my jokes? It was my turn to seek answers and discover who Delatron Kelley really was. I might have been alone, but I was *"Fighting to Win!"*

Made in United States
Orlando, FL
31 August 2023

36596458R00064